AI In the Classroom Without Coding:

A Teacher's Guide to Practical, Ethical, and Engaging AI Use

By Dr. Natoshia Anderson

I0143179

Dedication

To every teacher who shows up, adapts, and keeps learning.
This book is for you. Your commitment to your students inspires
change far beyond the classroom walls.

Chapter 1 – Demystifying AI for Educators

Opening Hook

When my colleague, a veteran 4th-grade teacher, first heard about "AI in the classroom," she laughed and said,

"That's for the techies in the robotics lab, not for me."

Two weeks later, she was using AI to adapt her reading comprehension assignments for three different student levels in less time than it used to take her to write one version. She didn't touch a single line of code.

This chapter is about getting you to that *aha* moment, where AI shifts from something "for other people" to something you can use today.

What Exactly Is AI (Without the Tech Headache)

At its simplest, **Artificial Intelligence** is a computer program that can "learn" patterns from data and then make predictions, generate content, or solve problems.

If that sounds abstract, think about:

- **Autocomplete** in your email: AI guesses what you'll type next.
- **Spell check**: AI identifies and fixes errors.
- **Streaming recommendations**: Netflix or Spotify "learn" what you like and suggest similar content.

The difference today is that AI tools can now:

- Generate **original text** (like a quiz or story) in seconds.
- Adapt resources to different student levels instantly.
- Provide real-time feedback for students.

And they can do it all without you needing to understand code.

Common Myths (and the Truth Behind Them)

Myth	Reality
AI will replace teachers.	AI can save you time, but it cannot build relationships, mentor students, or adapt to a classroom's emotional needs. That is your superpower.
I need to be tech-savvy to use AI.	Many tools work like Google Docs or Microsoft Word, you just type your request.
AI is too risky for the classroom.	Risks exist, but with the right guidelines and ethical practices, AI can be safe and powerful.
Only STEM teachers benefit from AI.	AI can write history debates, generate art prompts, or create differentiated reading passages, which is useful in any subject.

AI vs. Traditional Ed Tech

Traditional Ed Tech: Tools like online gradebooks or pre-made quizzes. They follow fixed instructions.
AI Tools: Adapt and respond to your input, more like having a teaching assistant who can brainstorm with you, make custom resources, and tweak them instantly.

Think of traditional ed tech as a **calculator** and AI as a **personal tutor** you can consult anytime.

You're Already Using AI (Probably Without Realizing It)

If you've used:

- Google Translate for an ESL parent email
- Grammarly to clean up a lesson handout
- An adaptive learning platform that adjusts questions based on student answers

…you've already worked with AI. The leap to using classroom AI tools is smaller than you think.

Why This Matters for Teachers Now

1. **Time Savings** – Lesson planning, grading, and feedback can eat up hours every week. AI can give you some of that time back.
2. **Differentiation Made Easy** – Create resources for struggling learners, advanced students, and everyone in between without rewriting everything from scratch.
3. **Student Engagement** – Interactive activities, personalized learning paths, and creative projects get students invested.
4. **Inclusion** – AI tools can help you meet diverse needs in your classroom, from language barriers to learning differences.

Quick Win: Your First AI Experiment

Here's a safe, no-risk way to dip your toe in:

1. Open a free AI tool like ChatGPT, Perplexity, or Microsoft Copilot.
2. Type:

"Create a 5-question quiz for [subject/topic] at a [grade level] reading level."

3. Look at the output. Ask the AI to "make it easier" or "add a bonus challenge question."

You've just co-created with AI.

Teacher Reflection Prompt

Grab a sticky note and jot down:

- The one task you'd most like to *never* do from scratch again.
- How much time it takes you each week.

Keep it handy. We will revisit it in Chapter 10 when we map your first 30-day AI plan.

Key Takeaways from This Chapter

- AI is already in your life, it is not a distant, futuristic tool.
- You don't need to code to use AI effectively.
- The goal is not to replace you, it is to amplify your impact and reclaim your time.

Chapter 2 – Getting Started with No-Code AI Tools

Opening Hook

When most people hear "AI tools," they picture lines of code scrolling on a screen or complicated software that requires hours of training. No-code AI tools work just like the programs you already use every day. If you can type in a search box or click a menu, you can use them.

This chapter will guide you through selecting your first AI tool, setting it up, and completing your first task in less than 15 minutes.

What Does No-Code Mean?

No-code means you do not have to program anything to make the tool work. Instead of learning a programming language, you use everyday language to tell the tool what you want.

Think of it like ordering food at a restaurant. You do not need to know the recipe or the cooking techniques. You just tell the server what you want, and the kitchen takes care of the rest.

Choosing the Right AI Tool for You

When selecting your first tool, consider three things:

1. **Purpose** – What do you want it to do? Lesson planning, grading assistance, generating activities, or creating student resources?
2. **Ease of Use** – Does it have a simple interface with clear instructions? Can you start without reading a manual?

3. **Cost and Access** – Many AI tools have a free version. Look for one that offers what you need without locking essential features behind a paywall.

Teacher-Friendly No-Code AI Tools to Try

- **ChatGPT** (Free and paid versions) – Great for lesson ideas, worksheets, quizzes, and writing prompts.
- **Perplexity AI** (Free) – A research-focused AI that includes citations and can simplify complex topics.
- **Canva Magic Studio** (Free and paid) – Can generate worksheets, infographics, and presentations from simple prompts.
- **Curipod** (Free) – Creates interactive lessons, polls, and quizzes.
- **Diffit** (Free) – Adapts reading materials to different grade levels.

Setting Up Your First Tool

1. **Choose one tool** from the list above.
2. Go to the website or app store and sign up with your school email or personal email.
3. Verify your account if required.
4. Spend no more than 5 minutes exploring the menu or features. Do not try to master everything right away.

Your First AI Task (15 Minutes or Less)

Example Prompt:

"Create a 10-minute interactive activity to introduce [topic] for [grade level] students."

Once you get the result:

- Review it for accuracy and relevance.
- Adjust the instructions if needed, for example: "Make it simpler for struggling readers" or "Add a discussion question."
- Test it with one student group and note their reactions.

Pro Tip: Be Specific in Your Requests

The more details you give, the better the output. Include:

- Grade level
- Subject and topic
- Desired format (quiz, game, worksheet)
- Learning goals

Example:

"Create a 5-question multiple-choice quiz on the water cycle for 5th-grade students, including one bonus challenge question, and provide an answer key."

Avoiding Overwhelm

You do not need to try every tool at once. Start with one, master it, and then expand. Adding too many tools too soon will make it harder to evaluate what is truly helping you.

Quick Win Activity

Pick one task from your teaching week that you do repeatedly. Use a no-code AI tool to complete it for you. Compare the time it took with your usual method.

Teacher Reflection Prompt

Write down:

- The tool you chose
- The task you completed
- How much time it saved you
- Any adjustments you needed to make to the AI's output

Key Takeaways from This Chapter

- No-code AI tools are accessible and simple to start using.
- Choosing the right tool depends on your purpose, ease of use, and cost.
- Start with one tool and one task to avoid overwhelm.

Chapter 3 – Lesson Planning Made Simple

Opening Hook

Lesson planning is one of the most time-consuming parts of teaching. By the time you write objectives, align standards, create activities, and design assessments, the hours have disappeared. AI can give you some of that time back while still allowing you to maintain full control over the quality and tone of your lessons.

This chapter will walk you through using AI to create lesson plans that are aligned with your standards, tailored to your students, and ready to implement faster than ever before.

Why AI Works for Lesson Planning

AI tools can:

- Generate a full lesson outline in seconds.
- Suggest multiple activities for different learning levels.
- Adjust the complexity or tone of content instantly.
- Provide fresh ideas when you feel stuck or uninspired.

The key is to see AI as a co-planner, not a replacement for your professional judgment.

Aligning AI Lessons to Your Curriculum Standards

When you create a lesson with AI, make sure it matches your state or national standards. You can include the standard in your request to help the AI align its output more closely to your requirements.

Example Prompt:

"Create a 45-minute 8th-grade science lesson on photosynthesis aligned with the Georgia Standards of Excellence, including a hands-on activity and a short formative assessment."

Differentiation Made Simple

AI can adjust one lesson to meet multiple needs:

- **For advanced learners:** Ask for extension activities or deeper research prompts.
- **For struggling learners:** Request simplified vocabulary and extra practice questions.
- **For mixed-ability groups:** Create tiered activities that allow students to choose their level of challenge.

Example Prompt:

"Take the above photosynthesis lesson and adapt it for 5th-grade students reading two grade levels below, keeping the activity hands-on."

Step-by-Step: Your First AI Lesson Plan

1. **Choose a topic** from your upcoming unit.
2. Open your AI tool and type a specific prompt with:
   - Grade level
   - Subject and topic
   - Standards or objectives
   - Activity type (hands-on, discussion-based, multimedia)
3. Review the AI's lesson plan. Highlight what works, cross out what does not, and adjust as needed.

4. Save the final version and add it to your planning binder or LMS.

Case Study: From One Hour to Ten Minutes

Mrs. Lopez, a 7th-grade social studies teacher, usually spent an hour planning each lesson. Using AI, she:

- Generated an outline in 20 seconds.
- Requested three activity variations for different skill levels in 1 minute.
- Tweaked the vocabulary and examples to match her students in 8 minutes.
  Total planning time: 10 minutes. She used the remaining 50 minutes to prepare materials and plan group projects.

Checking for Accuracy

AI tools are powerful, but they can make mistakes. Always:

- Verify facts with a reliable source.
- Adjust examples so they are culturally relevant for your students.
- Ensure the pacing matches your actual class period.

Quick Win Activity

Pick a lesson you need to teach next week. Use AI to generate:

- A lesson outline
- Two differentiated activity options

- One formative assessment
Compare the time it took versus your normal process.

Teacher Reflection Prompt

Write down:

- How much time you saved
- How much of the AI's output you kept as-is
- Any improvements you made that the AI could not have known to include

---

Key Takeaways from This Chapter

- AI can help you create quality lesson plans faster without sacrificing alignment to standards.
- Differentiation becomes much easier when AI can adjust complexity instantly.
- You remain the decision-maker, using AI as a creative partner.

Chapter 4 – Grading, Feedback, and Assessment

Opening Hook

Grading can feel endless. Between assignments, quizzes, essays, and projects, teachers can easily spend entire evenings or weekends reviewing student work. AI can take on the repetitive parts of grading so you can focus on the parts that require your professional insight, like spotting patterns in student learning and giving personalized encouragement.

This chapter will show you how to use AI to streamline grading, speed up feedback, and make assessment data more actionable.

How AI Can Help with Grading

AI can:

- Check objective answers like multiple choice, fill-in-the-blank, and true/false instantly.
- Suggest scoring for short responses and essays based on rubrics you provide.
- Highlight recurring student errors to help guide reteaching.
- Create summary reports of class performance.

Creating and Using Rubrics with AI

You can provide AI with your grading criteria and have it use those to evaluate work.

Example Prompt:

"Using the following rubric, evaluate this 9th-grade persuasive essay and give a score for each category: argument strength, evidence quality, organization, and grammar. Provide a one-sentence improvement suggestion for each category."

By setting clear parameters, you maintain consistent and aligned grading that aligns with your expectations.

Speeding Up Feedback

AI can generate feedback that is constructive, specific, and student-friendly.

Example Prompt:

"Provide feedback for a 5th-grade science project on plant growth, focusing on what the student did well and one suggestion for improvement, in language that is encouraging and easy to understand."

You can then personalize the tone or add specific references to the student's work.

Identifying Classwide Trends

AI can analyze a batch of student responses and point out patterns, such as:

- Many students missing the same question.
- Common vocabulary misunderstandings.
- Skills that need reinforcement.

This information can inform your reteaching plans and help you adapt upcoming lessons.

Keeping the Human Touch

AI can speed up grading and generate feedback, but it cannot replace the personal connection students feel when they know you have read their work. Use AI as a first draft generator, then add your comments to make feedback meaningful.

Case Study: Saving Time and Stress

Mr. Taylor, a high school English teacher, used AI to grade short-answer responses for comprehension checks. AI scored the answers and flagged unclear ones. He reviewed only the flagged responses and added his comments. This cut his grading time in half, allowing him to provide more thoughtful feedback on essays and projects.

Quick Win Activity

Choose one set of student work from this week that is time-consuming to grade.

- Create a rubric if you do not already have one.
- Use AI to apply the rubric to the student work.
- Compare the AI-generated grades and feedback to what you would give.

Teacher Reflection Prompt

Write down:

- How accurate the AI's grading was
- How much time you saved
- Which parts you still needed to do yourself

Key Takeaways from This Chapter

- AI can handle repetitive grading tasks quickly and accurately when given clear criteria.
- Automated feedback saves time, but adding your own voice keeps it personal.
- Analyzing patterns in student work can guide your next instructional steps.

Chapter 5 – Keeping Students Engaged

Opening Hook

Even the best-planned lesson can fall flat if students are not interested or invested. AI can help you create engaging, interactive activities that capture student attention and encourage participation. Whether you are working with energetic first graders or reserved high school seniors, AI can provide ideas and materials tailored to your students' needs and interests.

Why Engagement Matters

Engaged students:

- Retain information longer.
- Participate more actively.
- Show greater persistence when challenged.

AI can be a powerful support in building this engagement because it can instantly generate activities that are interactive, relevant, and adaptable for different learning styles.

AI-Powered Engagement Ideas

1. **Gamified Learning**
   - AI can create quizzes, puzzles, or scavenger hunts based on your lesson topic.
   - Example Prompt:

     > "Create a 10-question multiple-choice quiz on the American Revolution for 8th-grade students, formatted like a trivia game with increasing difficulty."

2. **Storytelling and Roleplay**
    - AI can generate short stories or scenarios for students to act out or respond to.
    - Example Prompt:

        > "Write a short, humorous story about a time-traveling mathematician who visits ancient Egypt, for 6th-grade students. Include three math challenges the character must solve."

3. **Creative Project Starters**
    - AI can suggest unique project ideas or starting points.
    - Example Prompt:

        > "Suggest five project ideas for high school biology students studying ecosystems, each with a hands-on component."

4. **Visual and Multimedia Aids**
    - Use AI-powered design tools like Canva Magic Studio to create infographics, posters, or slides.
    - Example Prompt:

        > "Create an infographic explaining the life cycle of a butterfly for 3rd-grade students using simple language and colorful visuals."

Adapting for Different Learning Styles

- **Visual learners:** Infographics, diagrams, and charts.
- **Auditory learners:** AI-generated podcasts, dialogues, or audio summaries.
- **Kinesthetic learners:** AI-designed hands-on activities or experiments.

When you identify the dominant learning styles in your class, you can tailor AI prompts to meet those needs.

Keeping Students Involved in the Process

You can involve students in creating activities by letting them brainstorm AI prompts with you. This not only boosts engagement but also helps them learn how to use AI responsibly.

Example:
During a unit on world geography, have students help create quiz questions by asking AI:

"Write five multiple-choice questions about the countries of South America, suitable for 7th-grade students."

Case Study: Turning a Dry Topic into an Interactive Experience

Ms. Howard was teaching cell biology, a unit her 9th-grade students found boring. She used AI to create a "Cell City" roleplay where each part of the cell became a character in a city. Students worked in groups to create skits introducing each character and its job. Engagement and test scores both improved.

Quick Win Activity

Choose a lesson topic you will teach this week.

- Use AI to generate one interactive activity related to that topic.
- Try it in class and observe student reactions.

- Adjust based on their engagement level.

Teacher Reflection Prompt

Write down:

- Which activity format your students responded to most
- How AI helped you create or improve it
- Any ideas for extending the activity

Key Takeaways from This Chapter

- Engagement increases learning retention and participation.
- AI can create a variety of interactive activities quickly.
- Involving students in AI-assisted activity creation deepens their connection to the content.

Chapter 6 – AI for Inclusion and Accessibility

Opening Hook

Every classroom has students with unique needs, abilities, and backgrounds. Meeting these needs can be one of the most rewarding parts of teaching, but it can also be one of the most time-consuming. AI can help you create materials and strategies that make learning more accessible and inclusive for every student, without doubling your workload.

Why Inclusion and Accessibility Matter

An inclusive classroom ensures that:

- All students can access the content, regardless of ability level or language background.
- Lessons are adapted to different strengths, challenges, and interests.
- Every student has an equal opportunity to succeed.

AI can make it easier to personalize lessons and remove barriers to learning, especially for special education, ESL, and diverse learning styles.

AI Strategies for Special Education

1. **Simplifying Language**
   - AI can rewrite complex text at a lower reading level without changing the meaning.
   - Example Prompt:

> "Rewrite this passage on the water cycle at a 3rd-grade reading level, keeping key vocabulary terms."

2. **Providing Multiple Formats**
   - Generate text, audio, and visual versions of lesson content.
   - Example Prompt:

     > "Create an audio script explaining the American Civil War for students with visual impairments."

3. **Breaking Down Steps**
   - AI can chunk large assignments into smaller, manageable parts with clear instructions.
   - Example Prompt:

     > "Break down the steps for writing a persuasive essay into five short, easy-to-follow tasks for middle school students."

AI Strategies for English as a Second Language (ESL) Students

1. **Translation Support**
   - AI tools can translate handouts, instructions, and feedback into a student's native language.
   - Example Prompt:

     > "Translate these classroom rules into Spanish and simplify the language for a 5th-grade reading level."

2. **Vocabulary Building**

- Generate glossaries with definitions, pictures, and examples.
- Example Prompt:

  > "Create a bilingual vocabulary list for key terms in a 7th-grade life science unit, including a simple definition and example sentence for each term."

3. **Language Practice Activities**
   - AI can create conversation prompts, fill-in-the-blank exercises, and pronunciation guides.

Making Materials More Accessible for All

- **Visual Learners:** Use AI to generate diagrams, charts, and labeled illustrations.
- **Auditory Learners:** Create audio summaries, podcasts, or discussion scripts.
- **Kinesthetic Learners:** Ask AI for ideas on interactive or hands-on activities that match your lesson objectives.

Case Study: Supporting Multiple Needs in One Lesson

Mr. Daniels, a high school history teacher, was preparing a lesson on the Great Depression. Using AI, he created:

- A simplified reading for struggling readers.
- A bilingual glossary for ESL students.
- A timeline graphic for visual learners.
- A roleplay activity for kinesthetic learners.

This approach ensured that all students could engage meaningfully with the material.

Quick Win Activity

Take one upcoming lesson and identify one barrier that might prevent a student from fully participating. Use AI to create a resource or adaptation that addresses that barrier.

Teacher Reflection Prompt

Write down:

- The barrier you addressed
- The AI-generated solution
- How the student responded

Key Takeaways from This Chapter

- AI can simplify, adapt, and translate materials to meet diverse student needs.
- Accessibility is about providing multiple ways for students to access the same learning goals.
- Inclusive classrooms are stronger when resources are adapted for all learners, not just some.

Chapter 7 – Ethical AI Use in Education

Opening Hook

AI can be a game-changer for your classroom, but without clear boundaries, it can also introduce risks you do not want to take. Responsible use is not just about avoiding trouble — it is about protecting your students, your professional integrity, and your school's reputation.

This chapter will walk you through the key ethical considerations for using AI in your teaching, along with practical steps you can take to keep your classroom safe and compliant.

Why Ethics Matters in AI Use

When you use AI in education, you are dealing with:

- **Student privacy** — ensuring personal information is not shared or stored unsafely.
- **Content bias** — making sure AI-generated material is fair, accurate, and inclusive.
- **Trust** — showing parents, administrators, and students that AI is used to help, not harm.

Ethical use builds confidence in your teaching practices and in the tools you choose.

Protecting Student Privacy

1. **Do Not Share Personal Data**
   - Avoid entering student names, addresses, grades, or identifying information into AI tools.

      o   If you need to use examples, replace real names with initials or generic placeholders.

2. **Understand Data Storage**
   - Check the privacy policy of any AI tool you use.
   - Ask: Does it store inputs? Is the data used to train the AI used for further training? Who can access it?

3. **Use School-Approved Tools**
   - Your district may already have a list of approved platforms that meet legal requirements like FERPA or COPPA.

Avoiding Bias in AI Content

1. **Review All AI-Generated Material**
   - AI can unintentionally create biased or culturally insensitive examples.
   - Always read and revise outputs before using them with students.

2. **Diversify Prompts**
   - Encourage the AI to include perspectives from different cultures, genders, and experiences.
   - Example Prompt:

     > "Create three historical case studies on the Industrial Revolution, including perspectives from workers, women, and people in colonized countries."

Following School and District Policies

1. **Check Existing Guidelines**
   - Many districts are creating AI usage policies for teachers.

- o Make sure your AI use aligns with those policies and update your practices as policies evolve.
2. **Model Responsible Use for Students**
   - o Discuss openly when and how you use AI.
   - o Show students the value of verifying AI information with reliable sources.

Communicating with Stakeholders

Parents and administrators may have concerns about AI.

- Be transparent about what tools you use and why.
- Provide examples of how AI saves time, personalizes learning, or improves accessibility.
- Share the safeguards you use to protect student information.

Case Study: Building Trust Through Openness

Ms. Ray, a middle school teacher, started using AI to help plan writing prompts. She explained her process to her students, demonstrated how she checked the AI's work for accuracy, and shared her AI usage guidelines with parents at open house. The transparency helped everyone feel comfortable with her approach.

Quick Win Activity

Write three personal AI classroom rules that focus on privacy, accuracy, and respect. Post them in your classroom or include them in your syllabus.

Teacher Reflection Prompt

Write down:

- One step you can take today to make your AI use more ethical
- How you will explain your AI use to students and parents

Key Takeaways from This Chapter

- Ethics in AI use is about protecting privacy, preventing bias, and building trust.
- Review all AI content before sharing it with students.
- Be transparent and follow district or school guidelines for technology use.

Chapter 8 – Academic Integrity and AI

Opening Hook

When students discover AI tools that can write essays, solve math problems, or generate reports in seconds, the temptation to skip the work can be strong. As teachers, we want students to use AI as a learning aid, not as a shortcut that undermines their education.

This chapter will help you set clear expectations, identify AI misuse, and guide students toward responsible, ethical AI habits.

Why Academic Integrity Matters with AI

- It ensures students actually learn the skills they need.
- It teaches honesty, accountability, and respect for intellectual property.
- It preserves the credibility of your assignments and grading.

If students rely on AI to do all their thinking, they miss the opportunity to develop critical skills they will need later in school and life.

Setting Classroom Guidelines for AI Use

1. **Be Explicit About What Is Allowed**
   - Define clearly when AI can be used and for what purposes.
   - Example: "You may use AI to brainstorm ideas for your essay, but you must write the essay yourself."
2. **Require Transparency**
   - Ask students to note in their work if and how they used AI.

- o Example: "Portions of the research outline were generated using ChatGPT and revised by me."
3. **Teach AI Literacy**
   - o Show students the strengths and limitations of AI so they understand why it should not be their only source.

Recognizing AI-Generated Student Work

1. **Look for Sudden Changes in Writing Style**
   - o If a student's work suddenly shifts to an advanced vocabulary and sentence structure that is not typical for them, it may be AI-generated.
2. **Use AI-Detection Tools (Cautiously)**
   - o Tools like GPTZero or Originality.ai can flag AI-generated text, but they are not always accurate. Use them as one data point, not the only proof.
3. **Ask Process Questions**
   - o Have students explain their reasoning or the steps they took to create their work. This can quickly reveal whether they actually understand the material.

Teaching Responsible AI Use

1. **Model How to Use AI Ethically**
   - o Show examples of how you use AI for planning or brainstorming and explain how you verify and adapt the results.
2. **Focus on Skills AI Cannot Replace**
   - o Emphasize critical thinking, personal reflection, creativity, and collaboration.
3. **Integrate AI into Assignments**

- Instead of banning AI entirely, create tasks where students compare AI-generated work to their own or fact-check AI's output.

Case Study: Turning a Problem into a Lesson

Mr. Harris discovered that several students in his history class had used AI to write their essays. Instead of giving zeros, he used it as a teaching moment. Students had to annotate the AI-generated essays, highlight inaccuracies, and revise them into accurate, original work. This approach reinforced both academic integrity and research skills.

Quick Win Activity

Create a one-page "AI Use in This Class" handout for students and parents. Include:

- When AI is permitted
- How to document AI use
- Consequences for misuse

Teacher Reflection Prompt

Write down:

- One change you can make to an assignment to encourage responsible AI use
- How you will teach students to verify AI-generated information

Key Takeaways from This Chapter

- Academic integrity with AI starts with clear expectations and transparency.
- Detection tools can help, but teacher judgment is essential.
- Responsible AI use can be taught through modeling and integration, not just restriction.

Chapter 9 – Building Trust with Parents and Administrators

Opening Hook

Even if you are confident in your use of AI, some parents and administrators may still be skeptical. Concerns about privacy, academic integrity, and the role of technology in learning are common. By being transparent, proactive, and clear about your goals, you can build trust and gain the support you need to use AI effectively in your classroom.

Why Building Trust Matters

When stakeholders understand how and why you use AI, they are more likely to:

- Support your teaching strategies.
- Advocate for the tools you need.
- See AI as a positive addition to the learning process rather than a threat.

Common Concerns About AI in Education

1. **Privacy** – Will my child's personal information be safe?
2. **Overreliance** – Will AI replace critical thinking and creativity?
3. **Accuracy** – Can AI produce incorrect or biased content?
4. **Equity** – Will all students benefit equally, or will some be left out?

Acknowledging these concerns early shows that you take them seriously.

Communicating with Parents

1. **Explain Your Purpose**
   - Share why you are using AI, whether it is to save time, differentiate instruction, or enhance engagement.
2. **Show Examples**
   - Provide AI-generated lesson ideas, quizzes, or activity prompts so parents can see the quality and type of output you use.
3. **Share Safeguards**
   - Explain your privacy practices and how you review AI content before using it with students.
4. **Invite Dialogue**
   - Encourage parents to ask questions or share concerns in meetings, emails, or open houses.

Communicating with Administrators

1. **Link to School Goals**
   - Align your AI use with district or school initiatives, such as personalized learning, technology integration, or inclusion.
2. **Provide Evidence of Impact**
   - Share data on time saved, improved student engagement, or performance gains.
3. **Offer to Share Practices**
   - Be a resource for other teachers who want to explore AI responsibly.

Practical Communication Tools

- **Parent Letter Template**

  > "In our classroom, we use AI as a supportive tool to create activities, adapt materials for different learners, and save time on routine tasks. All content is reviewed before use, and no student personal information is shared with AI platforms. Students are encouraged to use AI responsibly, as a learning aid rather than a replacement for their own work."

- **Administrator Report Template**
  Include:
  - Purpose of AI use
  - Tools used
  - Safeguards in place
  - Measurable results (time saved, increased engagement, improved access for diverse learners)

Case Study: Winning Over Skeptics

Mrs. Patel faced pushback from a few parents when she introduced AI activities. She invited them to observe a lesson where students used AI to brainstorm ideas for a group project, then developed and presented their own work. Parents saw firsthand that students were still doing the thinking, and concerns quickly faded.

Quick Win Activity

Draft a short paragraph that explains your AI approach in plain language. Share it with a colleague and ask if it feels clear, reassuring, and confident.

Teacher Reflection Prompt

Write down:

- One way you can be more transparent about your AI use with parents
- One way you can demonstrate AI's positive impact to administrators

---

Key Takeaways from This Chapter

- Transparency builds trust and reduces skepticism.
- Address privacy, accuracy, and overreliance concerns directly.
- Share examples and results to show that AI is a support, not a substitute, for teaching.

Chapter 10 – Your First 30 Days with AI

Opening Hook

Starting with AI can be both exciting and a bit overwhelming. There are countless tools, features, and possibilities to explore. The best way to build confidence is to start small, make progress in stages, and track your wins. This 30-day plan will help you integrate AI into your teaching in a way that is sustainable and effective.

Week 1: Pick One Tool and One Task

Goal: Get comfortable with a single AI platform.

- Choose one no-code AI tool from earlier chapters, such as ChatGPT, Perplexity AI, or Canva Magic Studio.
- Select one task you do regularly, like creating quiz questions, drafting lesson outlines, or generating vocabulary lists.
- Use AI to complete that task once this week.
- Evaluate the results: Was it accurate? Did it save you time? Was it easy to edit for your class?

Example Prompt:

"Create a 10-question multiple-choice quiz on the causes of the American Revolution for 8th-grade students, with an answer key."

Week 2: Add a Lesson Planning Use Case

Goal: Expand AI use to planning a single lesson.

- Choose an upcoming topic and use AI to generate a full lesson outline.
- Include standards, learning objectives, and at least one differentiated activity.
- Review and adapt the plan for your students.
- Teach the lesson and note student engagement levels.

Example Prompt:

"Create a 45-minute 5th-grade science lesson on the phases of the moon, aligned to the Next Generation Science Standards, with an activity for visual learners and one for kinesthetic learners."

Week 3: Introduce a Student-Facing Activity

Goal: Let students interact with AI-generated content.

- Use AI to create an interactive activity, such as a trivia game, roleplay scenario, or group challenge.
- Keep the activity short and low stakes to focus on engagement.
- Explain to students how you used AI to create it and how it supports their learning.

Example Prompt:

"Create a short mystery story for 4th-grade students where they must solve clues about animal habitats."

Week 4: Reflect, Adjust, and Expand

Goal: Evaluate your experience and decide on your next steps.

- Review your AI uses over the past month.

- Identify the biggest time-saving or engagement-boosting results.
- Decide whether to add a second tool or a new type of task, such as grading support or accessibility adaptations.

Questions to Ask Yourself:

- Which AI activities worked best?
- What needed the most editing?
- How did students respond?
- What will you try next month?

Tracking Your Wins

Keep a simple log of:

- Tasks completed with AI
- Time saved compared to your normal process
- Student engagement ratings (even informal ones)
- Any feedback from students, parents, or administrators

This record will be helpful for your own reflection, and it can also be shared with administrators to demonstrate the value of your approach.

Case Study: From Hesitant to Confident in 30 Days

Mr. Lopez, a 6th-grade math teacher, started by using AI to create warm-up problems once a week. By the end of the month, he had used AI for lesson outlines, differentiated practice sets, and a classroom math competition. His students were more engaged, and he reported saving over three hours a week in planning time.

Quick Win Activity

Create your own 30-day AI plan. Choose your first tool, your first task, and your first student-facing activity. Commit to reflecting and adjusting each week.

Teacher Reflection Prompt

Write down:

- The tool you will start with
- The first task you will try
- One student-facing activity you will introduce

Key Takeaways from This Chapter

- Start small and build your skills gradually.
- Track time saved and student impact to guide your next steps.
- A month is enough to go from curious to confident with AI in your classroom.

Conclusion: AI as Your Teaching Partner

You began this journey learning what AI is and how it can fit into your teaching without requiring a single line of code. You explored tools, strategies, ethical considerations, and step-by-step ways to integrate AI into your classroom.

By now, you have seen that AI is not a replacement for you — it is a partner that can save you time, spark creativity, and help you meet the diverse needs of your students.

The real power of AI in education comes from the teacher who uses it. You bring the human judgment, empathy, and understanding that no machine can replicate. AI simply gives you more space to focus on those human strengths.

Your next step is simple: choose one strategy from this book and try it this week. Reflect on how it works, refine it, and then expand from there. Progress happens one step at a time.

You do not need to master everything at once. You just need to start.

Resources for Teachers

AI Tools for Educators (No-Code)

1. **ChatGPT** – General content creation, lesson ideas, quizzes.
   Website: https://chat.openai.com
2. **Perplexity AI** – Research with citations and simplified explanations.
   Website: https://perplexity.ai

3. **Canva Magic Studio** – Visuals, worksheets, and presentations from prompts.
   Website: https://www.canva.com/magic-studio
4. **Curipod** – Interactive lessons, polls, and quizzes.
   Website: https://curipod.com
5. **Diffit** – Adapts reading materials to different grade levels.
   Website: https://diffit.me

AI Accessibility & Inclusion Tools

1. **NaturalReader** – Text-to-speech for reading support.
   Website: https://www.naturalreaders.com
2. **Read&Write by Texthelp** – Reading, writing, and translation assistance.
   Website: https://www.texthelp.com
3. **Microsoft Immersive Reader** – Built-in accessibility features for reading and comprehension.
   Website: https://learn.microsoft.com/en-us/education/tools/immersive-reader

---

AI Detection & Academic Integrity Tools

1. **GPTZero** – Detects AI-generated text (use cautiously).
   Website: https://gptzero.me
2. **Originality.ai** – Checks for plagiarism and AI writing.
   Website: https://originality.ai

Professional Development Resources

1. **ISTE AI in Education Resources** – Guidelines and PD for teachers.
   Website: https://iste.org

2. **Edutopia** – Articles and ideas for AI integration.
   Website: https://www.edutopia.org
3. **KQED MindShift** – Education news and innovative teaching strategies.
   Website: https://www.kqed.org/mindshift

Templates and Checklists (Printable)

- AI Lesson Plan Prompt Template
- AI Grading & Feedback Checklist
- AI Classroom Rules Poster
- AI Parent Letter Template
- 30-Day AI Implementation Tracker

Final Encouragement

You do not have to be a tech expert to bring the benefits of AI into your classroom. You just have to be willing to try, reflect, and grow.

Your students will benefit not only from the efficiency AI offers you, but also from the example you set in using new tools with thoughtfulness, responsibility, and creativity.

The future of education is not about replacing teachers with machines — it is about empowering teachers with better tools. And now, you have everything you need to take the first step.

www.ingramcontent.com/pod-product-compliance
Lightning Source LLC
LaVergne TN
LVHW051430080426
835508LV00022B/3338